PUFFIN FACTFINDER

FANTASTIC
SEA CREATURES

Written by
Rupert Matthews

Consultant
Laura Wade

Edited by
Hazel Songhurst

PUFFIN BOOKS

The author, Rupert Matthews, is a freelance writer and established author of information books for children.

The consultant, Laura Wade, has been Educational Services Manager for the UK Sea Life Centres. She is currently managing a Nature Park project.

PUFFIN BOOKS

Published by the Penguin Group
Penguin Books Ltd. , 27 Wrights Lane, London W8 5TZ, England
Penguin Books USA Inc, 375 Hudson Street, New York, New York 10014, USA
Penguin Books Australia Ltd, Ringwood, Victoria, Australia
Penguin Books Canada Ltd, 10 Alcorn Avenue, Toronto, Ontario, Canada M4V 3B2
Penguin Books (NZ) Ltd, 182-190 Wairau Road, Auckland 10, New Zealand

Penguin Books Ltd, Registered Offices: Harmondsworth, Middlesex, England

First published 1995
10 9 8 7 6 5 4 3 2 1

Produced for Puffin Books by Zigzag Publishing Ltd, The Barn, Randolph's Farm, Brighton Road, Hurstpierpoint, West Sussex, BN6 9EL, England

Series concept: Tony Potter
Managing Editor: Nicola Wright
Editors: Kay Barnham & Hazel Songhurst
Design: Chris Leishman
Illustrators: Peter Bull, Mainline Design, Treve Tamblin (John Martin Artists) , Lee Gibbons, John Yates.
Cover Illustrator: Lee Gibbons
Production: Zoe Fawcett and Simon Eaton

Colour separations: Sussex Repro Ltd, England
Printed by: Proost, Belgium

Contents

About this book

Did you know that over three-quarters of the Earth's surface is covered by water? An amazing variety of fish and other animals live in the seas and oceans.

This book tells you about the colourful creatures that inhabit a coral reef, the strange fish that live in the dark sea-depths, about deadly sharks, and about sea-mammals, such as seals, dolphins and whales.

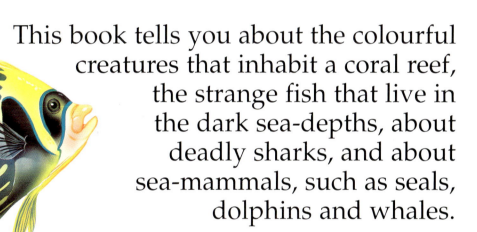

Find out, too, about underwater animals that lived millions of years ago and whether creatures such as sea-monsters and mermaids really existed.

Coral creatures

Coral reefs are made from millions of tiny creatures called coral polyps. When it dies, each polyp leaves behind a tiny limestone skeleton. There are thousands of types of polyp.

Many other creatures live on the reef. The shallow water and rocky crevices provide an ideal home.

The largest coral reef in the world is the **Great Barrier Reef** off the east coast of Queensland, Australia. It is over 2,000 km long.

The **sweetlips emperor** fish grows up to 1 metre long. Humans like to catch this tasty creature.

The **sea horse** feeds on shrimps. It can change colour to hide from enemies.

Unlike most fish, the **clown anemone fish** is immune to the sea anemone's poison. It hides in the creature's tentacles, safe from attack, whilst hunting for its prey.

Coral polyps need warm, clear water in which to grow. Their tentacles wave in the water to capture prey.

The **blue shark** cruises the reef, hunting for prey.

The **imperial angelfish** has bright stripes to match the colours of the coral.

A **lionfish** has bright stripes to warn other fish that its spines are poisonous.

Anemones use their tentacles to catch prey. Poisonous barbs kill the fish which are then pulled into the anemone's mouth.

The **stonefish** looks like a stone and hides in gaps in the reef. Any human who trod on its poisonous spines would die!

The **crown of thorns starfish** eats coral polyps. Usually, new polyps replace those eaten and the reef survives any damage.

Life on the shore can be very difficult for animals. As the tide comes in and goes out, their surroundings change from dry land to shallow sea.

Pounding waves throw animals around. The sand is always moving as the sea pushes and pulls it around. Seashore animals must be tough to survive.

Prawns feed among the seaweed. When the tide goes out, they swim into deeper water, but sometimes they are caught in rock pools.

The **scorpion fish** and other kinds of small fish feed among the stones in rock pools. They swim out with the tide.

The **masked crab** lives on sandy beaches. When the tide goes out, it burrows into the sand. The tips of its two antennae poke out of the sand and act as breathing tubes.

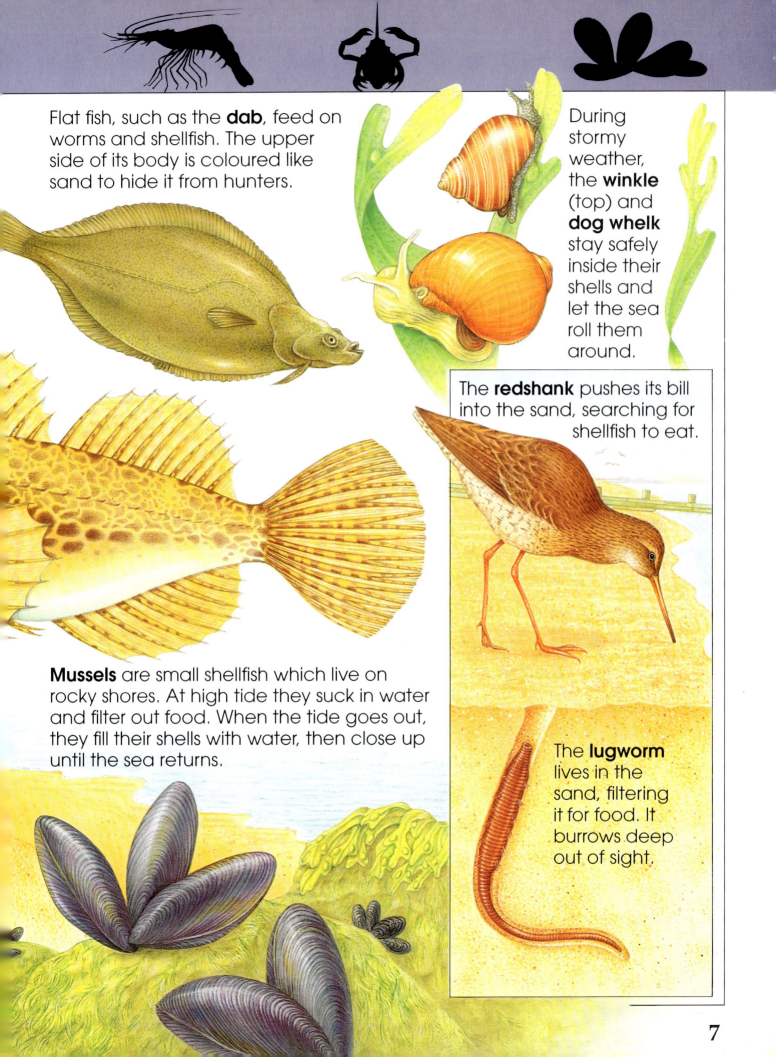

Flat fish, such as the **dab**, feed on worms and shellfish. The upper side of its body is coloured like sand to hide it from hunters.

During stormy weather, the **winkle** (top) and **dog whelk** stay safely inside their shells and let the sea roll them around.

The **redshank** pushes its bill into the sand, searching for shellfish to eat.

Mussels are small shellfish which live on rocky shores. At high tide they suck in water and filter out food. When the tide goes out, they fill their shells with water, then close up until the sea returns.

The **lugworm** lives in the sand, filtering it for food. It burrows deep out of sight.

Most sea creatures live near the surface, where the water is warm and sunlit. The light cannot travel very deep and the sea's currents rarely move the warm surface water down to the depths of the ocean.

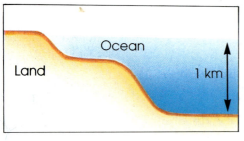

At depths of more than one kilometre, the sea is very cold and completely dark. Some very strange creatures live here. They feed on each other and on food which drifts down from above.

Sperm whales dive down for food.

The **giant squid** can grow to 20 metres long.

Deep-sea shrimps can glow to attract a mate.

The **deep-sea angler fish** has a long growth over its mouth which glows faintly. This attracts other fish, which are then swallowed whole!

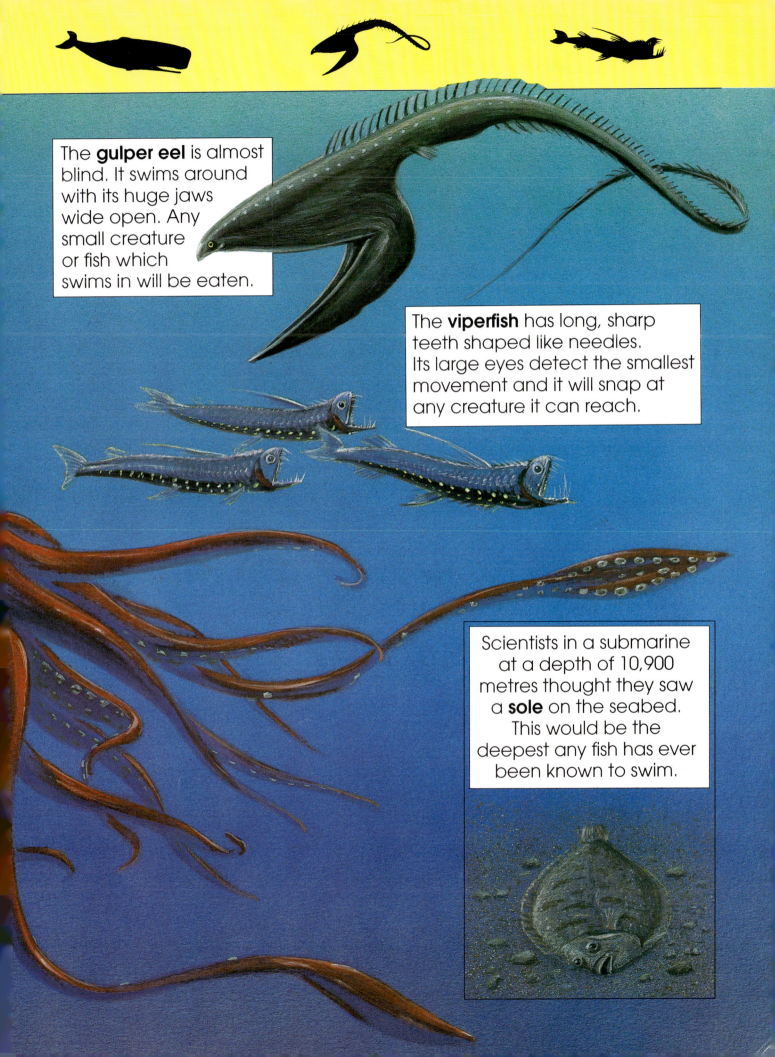

The **gulper eel** is almost blind. It swims around with its huge jaws wide open. Any small creature or fish which swims in will be eaten.

The **viperfish** has long, sharp teeth shaped like needles. Its large eyes detect the smallest movement and it will snap at any creature it can reach.

Scientists in a submarine at a depth of 10,900 metres thought they saw a **sole** on the seabed. This would be the deepest any fish has ever been known to swim.

Around both the North and South Poles, the weather is very cold. A layer of ice floats on top of the sea all year round.

Animals which live there must be able to keep warm. They may have thick fur, like the polar bear, or layers of fat under their skin, like the common seal.

Killer whales prey on any creatures they can catch. They will even push ice from underwater to knock penguins and seals into the sea.

Penguins are birds that live around the South Pole. They lay their eggs on the ice and hunt for fish in the sea.

The largest penguin is the **Emperor penguin** which grows to over 1 metre tall.

The smallest penguin is the **fairy penguin**, which is only 40 cm tall.

Seals live in the oceans around the North and South Poles. The **grey seal** grows up to 2.4 metres long. The **common seal** hunts for fish and squid in northern waters. The fierce **leopard seal** from the southern oceans hunts penguins as well as fish.

Grey seal

Common seal

Leopard seal

Cod

Haddock

Squid

Plankton

Beneath the ice live large numbers of **squid** and fish such as **cod** and **haddock**. They feed on tiny plants and animals, called **plankton**, which float in the water.

Polar bears live on the northern ice where they hunt seals, snow hares and other animals.

Polar bears can run faster than humans.

The smallest living things in the sea are called plankton. They are so small that you could fit 40,000 of them on the end of your thumb.

Plankton can be either plants or animals. They are food for the larger sea animals.

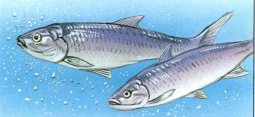

Large clouds of plankton drift in the surface waters of all seas.

Phyto-plankton are microscopic plants. They use the sunlight's energy to grow like plants on land.

The smallest animals are made of a single body-cell. **Ceratium** moves by thrashing a long, whip-like 'arm'. It feeds on tiny plants.

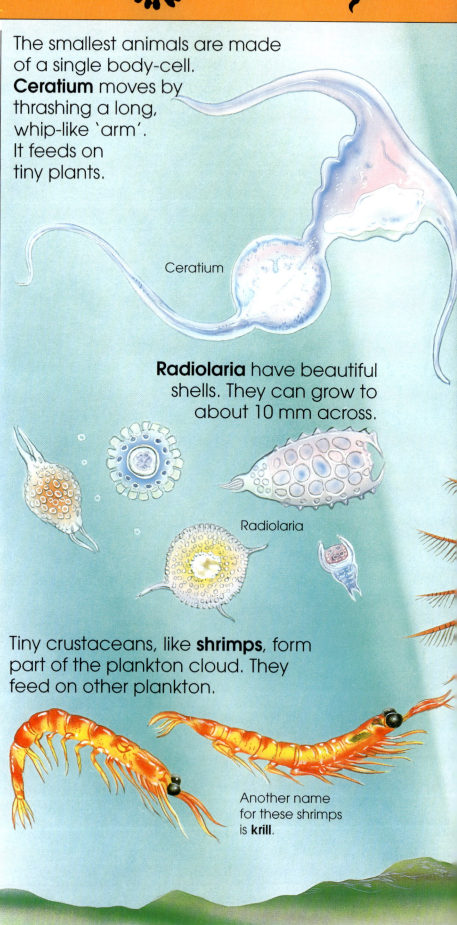

Ceratium

Radiolaria have beautiful shells. They can grow to about 10 mm across.

Radiolaria

Tiny crustaceans, like **shrimps**, form part of the plankton cloud. They feed on other plankton.

Another name for these shrimps is **krill**.

Some of the **plankton** are the young of much larger creatures. Because they drift with the ocean currents, these creatures can travel much further than they can as adults, allowing them to reach new homes.

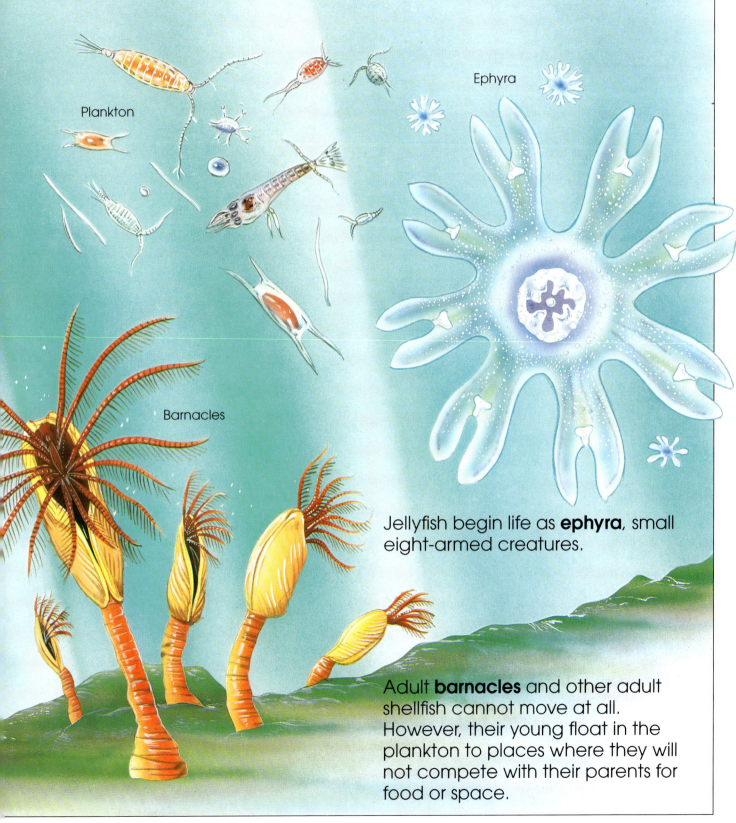

Plankton

Ephyra

Barnacles

Jellyfish begin life as **ephyra**, small eight-armed creatures.

Adult **barnacles** and other adult shellfish cannot move at all. However, their young float in the plankton to places where they will not compete with their parents for food or space.

13

Whales are mammals which have evolved to live in the sea. They have fins instead of legs and a powerful tail to push them through the water.

Like all mammals, whales breathe air, so they need to come to the surface from time to time.

The **bowhead whale's** head is 6 metres long. This is one-third of its length. The jaws are packed with baleen to filter food from the sea water.

The largest whales feed on plankton. They have special filters, called baleen, in their mouths which strain seawater and remove the tiny animals and plants to be eaten.

The earliest known whale is **basiliosaurus**, which lived about 40 million years ago.

The **sei whale** is 15 metres long. It is the fastest swimmer and can speed along at 50 kilometres an hour.

The **blue whale** is the largest whale of all. Over 30 metres in length, a really large blue whale may weigh 160 tonnes. Each blue whale eats four tonnes of plankton every day.

A newborn blue whale is the size of an elephant!

The 15-metre long **grey whale** lives in the Pacific Ocean. It travels almost 20,000 kilometres between its summer and winter feeding grounds.

Coastline creatures

Seals are mammals which have evolved to live in the oceans.

Their legs have become flippers to help them swim, but they can still move on land.

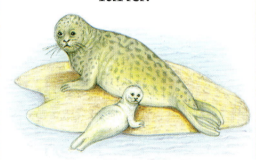

Seals spend some of their time on shore, either caring for their babies or resting from hunting for fish.

Elephant seals were once hunted for the rich oil their bodies contdin. At one time, only about a hundred were still alive, but today there are over 50,000 of them.

The **harp seal** hunts fish beneath the ocean surface. Thick layers of fat under its skin protect it from the icy water.

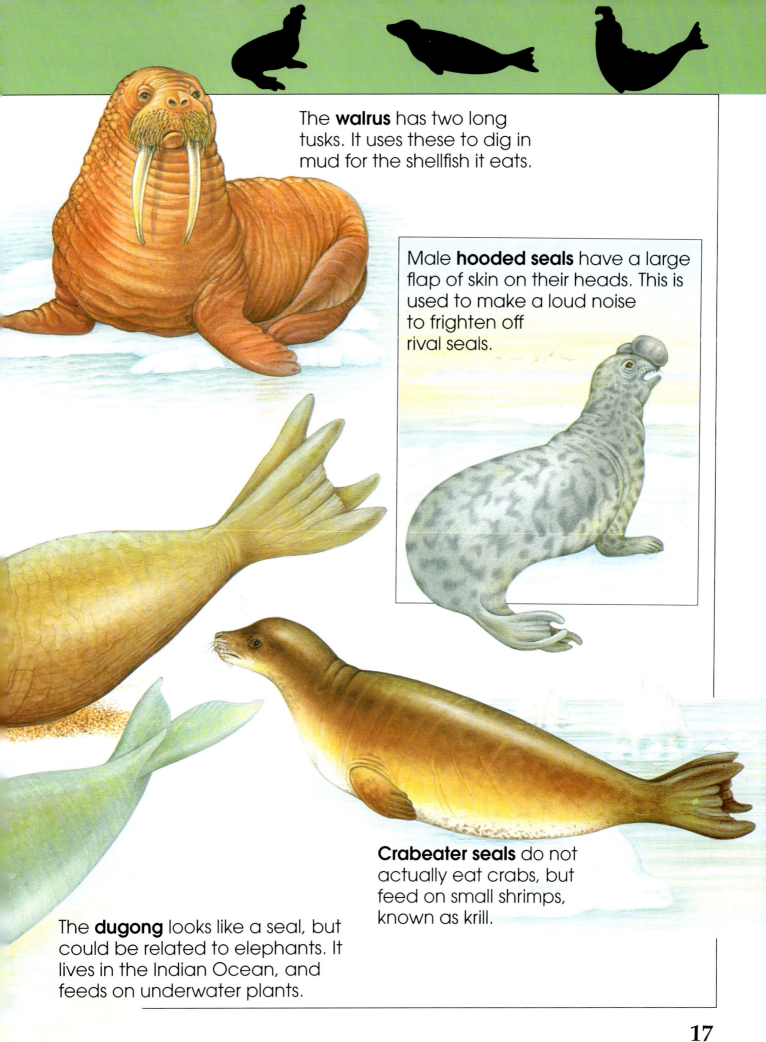

The **walrus** has two long tusks. It uses these to dig in mud for the shellfish it eats.

Male **hooded seals** have a large flap of skin on their heads. This is used to make a loud noise to frighten off rival seals.

Crabeater seals do not actually eat crabs, but feed on small shrimps, known as krill.

The **dugong** looks like a seal, but could be related to elephants. It lives in the Indian Ocean, and feeds on underwater plants.

Dolphins belong to a group of whales called toothed whales. They do not eat plankton but hunt squid and fish.

Dolphins are very intelligent creatures. They communicate with each other using different sounds arranged like words in a sentence.

Some dolphins are very rare. The **shepherd's beaked whale** is a recent discovery.

Dolphins are social animals. They live in family groups. If one dolphin is sick or injured, others will come to its rescue.

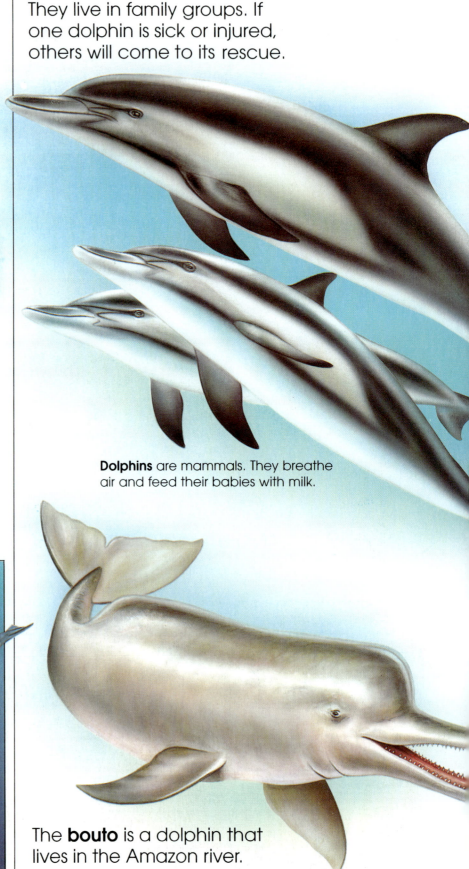

Dolphins are mammals. They breathe air and feed their babies with milk.

The **bouto** is a dolphin that lives in the Amazon river.

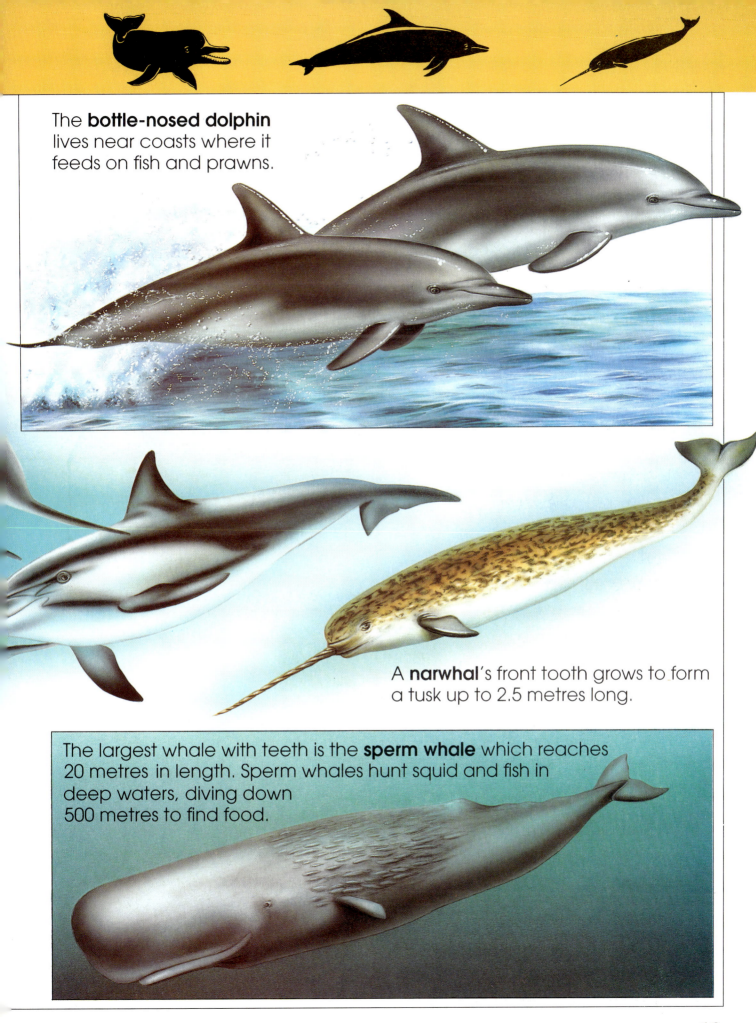

The **bottle-nosed dolphin** lives near coasts where it feeds on fish and prawns.

A **narwhal**'s front tooth grows to form a tusk up to 2.5 metres long.

The largest whale with teeth is the **sperm whale** which reaches 20 metres in length. Sperm whales hunt squid and fish in deep waters, diving down 500 metres to find food.

Deadly creatures

Sharks and rays are found in all seas. Their skeletons are made of soft cartilage instead of hard bone.

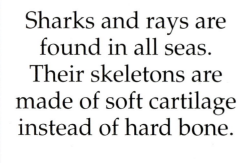

The largest shark is the 18-metre long **whale shark**. Unlike most sharks, it does not hunt other animals. Instead, it feeds on plankton.

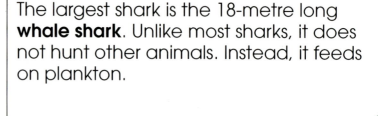

The harmless **whale shark** lives in warm waters.

Sharks hunt other sea creatures, using their sharp teeth and strong muscles to overpower their prey.

The **great white shark** sometimes attacks people.

The largest hunting shark is the **great white shark**. It may grow to 7 metres long and usually feeds on larger fish and other animals.

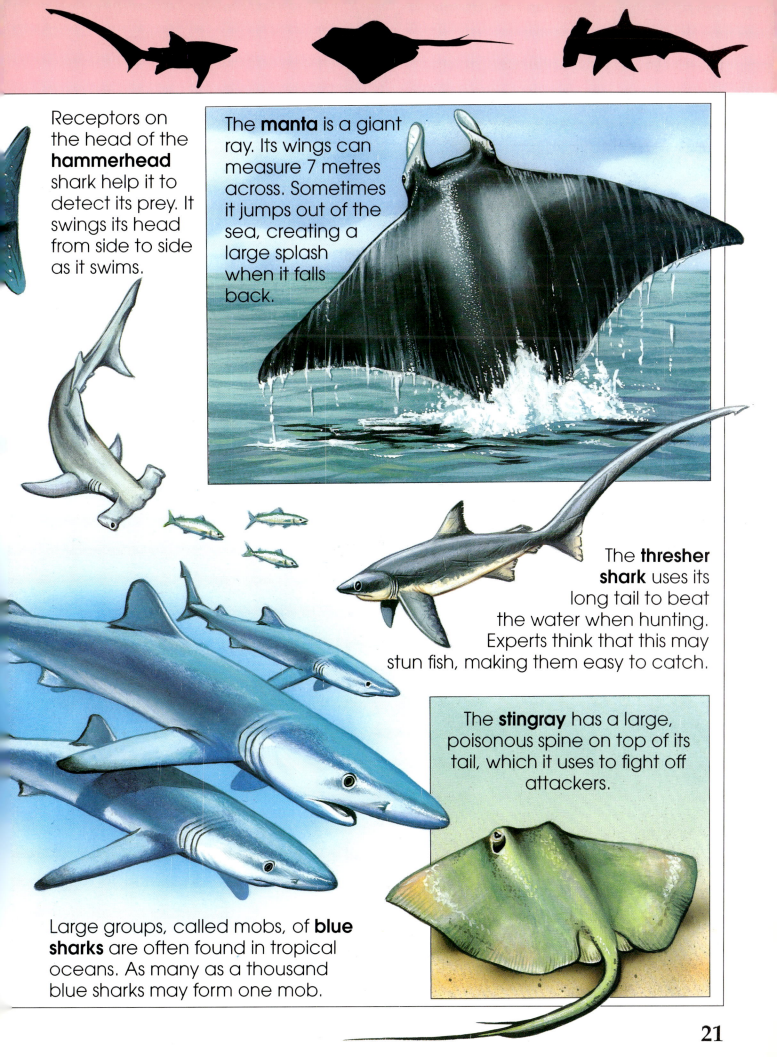

Receptors on the head of the **hammerhead** shark help it to detect its prey. It swings its head from side to side as it swims.

The **manta** is a giant ray. Its wings can measure 7 metres across. Sometimes it jumps out of the sea, creating a large splash when it falls back.

The **thresher shark** uses its long tail to beat the water when hunting. Experts think that this may stun fish, making them easy to catch.

The **stingray** has a large, poisonous spine on top of its tail, which it uses to fight off attackers.

Large groups, called mobs, of **blue sharks** are often found in tropical oceans. As many as a thousand blue sharks may form one mob.

Flying creatures

Many birds live at sea feeding on fish or other sea creatures.

Most seabirds nest on islands, where their eggs and young are safe from attack.

Seabirds often make long journeys between their nesting sites and feeding grounds. Arctic terns travel between the Arctic and the Antarctic.

The **great skua** is a large bird, over 50 cm long. It hunts other seabirds, as well as fish.

Herring gulls are very common. They feed on fish and shrimps, but will also fly inland to raid rubbish dumps and picnic areas.

A **skimmer** finds fish by flying just above the surface of the sea, with its bill in the water. As soon as the bill strikes a fish, it is snapped up.

The largest seabird is the **wandering albatross**, which has wings 3.5 metres across. Long ago, sailors believed it was bad luck to kill an albatross.

Steamer ducks live around the coast. They cannot fly, but swim along the shore looking for shellfish, shrimps and crabs to eat.

Puffins nest on cliffs and rocky islands. The females lay just one egg each year.

Gannet fly around searching for fish in the water. They may dive from a height of 30 metres to catch their prey.

Reptiles are animals such as lizards. Most live on land.

A few types of reptile have evolved to live in the ocean, but they need to come to the surface often to breathe air.

Most sea reptiles lay their eggs on dry land. They may come ashore once a year to do this.

The **green turtle** has a tough shell to protect it from attack. It feeds on seaweed and jellyfish.

The **leatherback turtle** has no shell, but the skin on its back is very thick and tough.

Estuary crocodiles live off the coasts of northern Australia. They can grow to be over 6 metres long and are the largest sea reptiles alive today.

Ridley turtles crunch up shellfish with their strong jaws.

The **banded sea snake** lives in the Pacific Ocean where it hunts fish. It is one of the most poisonous snakes in the world.

The **hawksbill turtle** is very rare. Not long ago, it was hunted for its shell. This was used to make things such as ornate boxes and spectacle frames.

Marine iguanas live around the remote Galapagos islands in the Pacific Ocean. They dive into the ocean to feed on seaweed.

Marine iguanas come ashore to bask in the sun.

Strange creatures

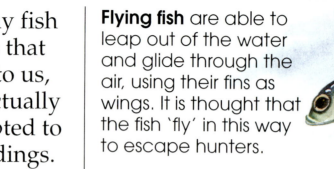

There are many fish in the oceans that look strange to us, but they are actually very well adapted to their surroundings.

Thousands of fish have evolved to live in different places - on coral reefs, in icy waters, near the surface of the sea, or on the sea-bed.

Flying fish are able to leap out of the water and glide through the air, using their fins as wings. It is thought that the fish 'fly' in this way to escape hunters.

When danger threatens, the **porcupine fish** gulps huge amounts of water and swells up to four times its usual size. The stiff spines stick out to make the fish look like a spiky football.

The **four-eyed fish** swims at the surface with each of its two eyes half in and half out of the water. The fish looks for insect prey on the surface, while watching for danger under the sea.

The **swordfish** has a bony upper jaw which can be over 1 metre long and shaped like a sword. Nobody knows what the sword is used for.

The **sailfish** is the fastest fish in the sea. It can reach speeds of 110 kilometres per hour.

The **coelacanth** lives in the deep waters of the Indian Ocean. Before it was caught in 1938, the coelacanth was known only from fossils dating back 60 million years. Scientists thought it had been extinct ever since.

Porcupine fish

The **sea dragon** is only 40 cm long. It swims near seaweed where it can hide easily.

Millions of years ago, strange creatures lived in the oceans.

Scientists know about these creatures because they have found fossils of their bones buried in ancient rocks.

Many of these giant sea animals lived at the same time as the dinosaurs.

Kronosaurus had the largest head of any hunter in the sea. It was almost 3 metres long and was armed with lots of sharp teeth.

Cryptocleidus had strong flippers to propel it through the water. It caught small fish in its long jaws armed with sharp teeth.

Ichthyosaurus looked like a dolphin or large fish, but was really a reptile. Ichthyosaurus could not come on shore to lay eggs like most reptiles, so it gave birth to live young.

Archelon was the largest turtle. It was nearly 4 metres long and lived about 70 million years ago.

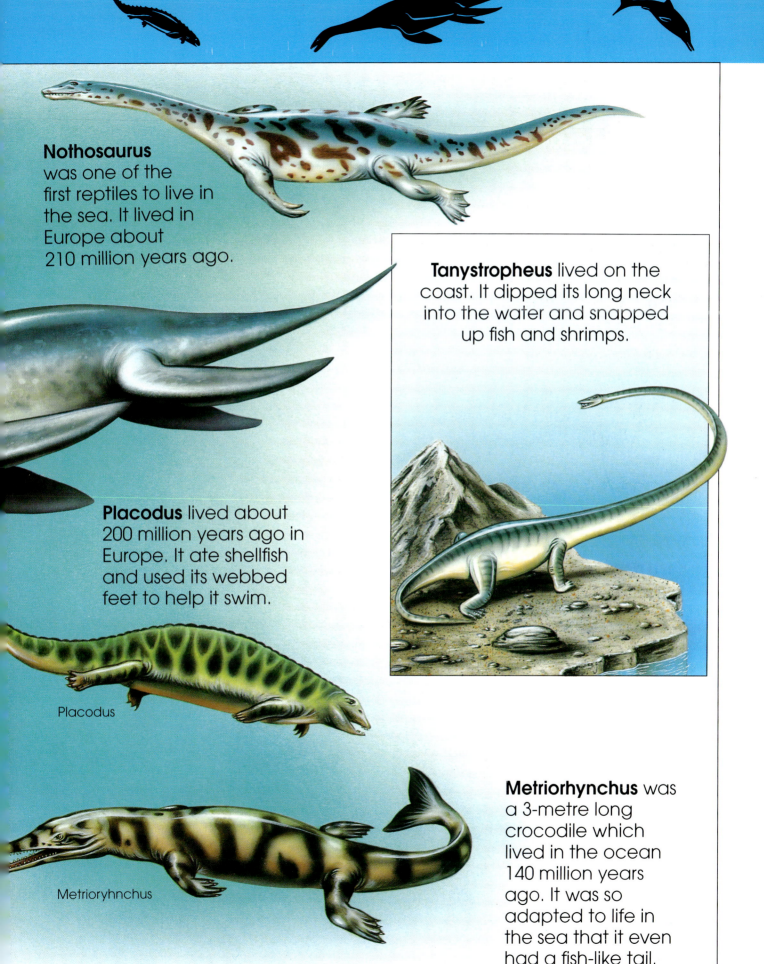

Nothosaurus was one of the first reptiles to live in the sea. It lived in Europe about 210 million years ago.

Tanystropheus lived on the coast. It dipped its long neck into the water and snapped up fish and shrimps.

Placodus lived about 200 million years ago in Europe. It ate shellfish and used its webbed feet to help it swim.

Placodus

Metrioryhnchus

Metriorhynchus was a 3-metre long crocodile which lived in the ocean 140 million years ago. It was so adapted to life in the sea that it even had a fish-like tail.

Because the oceans are so vast, there are many areas which have never been explored properly.

Sailors who have travelled off the main shipping routes have reported seeing strange and curious creatures. As nobody has ever caught one of these mysterious creatures, scientists do not believe they really exist.

The type of **sea monster** most often seen has a small head and a long neck held upright. Witnesses say they see a large body under the water with four large fins which move the creature slowly along.

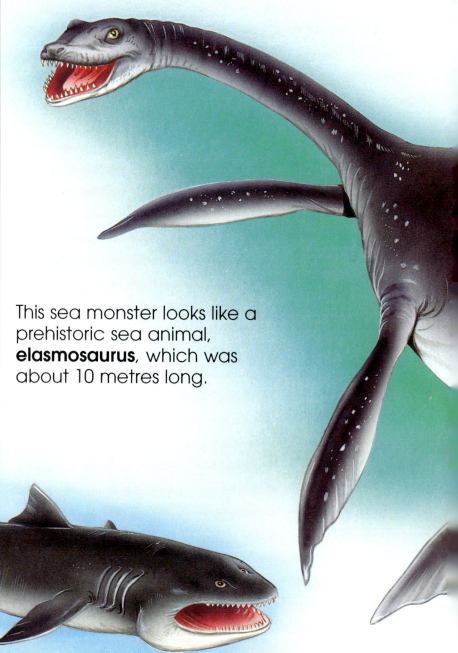

This sea monster looks like a prehistoric sea animal, **elasmosaurus**, which was about 10 metres long.

The 4-metre long **megamouth shark** was not discovered until the 1980s. Nobody knew about it until one was accidentally caught in a net. This proved that large sea creatures can exist without anybody knowing about them.

Manatees swim slowly in shallow coastal waters, feeding on water plants.

Long ago, sailors believed in **mermaids**. Today, scientists know that what they probably saw were seal-like creatures called **manatees**.

The **sea serpent** is supposed to be a gigantic, snake-like creature up to 30 metres long. Many people have reported seeing them.

A giant turtle-like creature was seen in 1877 by the crew of *HMS Osborne*. The creature was about 20 metres long and swam quickly.

Index